Infant Baptism and Adult Conversion

INFANT BAPTISM
AND
ADULT CONVERSION

By

O. HALLESBY

Translated from the Norwegian by
CLARENCE J. CARLSEN

AUGSBURG PUBLISHING HOUSE
Minneapolis, Minnesota

Contents

Introduction

THE relation between regeneration in Baptism on the one hand and awakening and conversion on the other is a problem which has produced great difficulties through the history of the church. This comes most clearly to light in the preaching. Some preaching keeps baptismal grace clearly in view and speaks of it both often and fervently. But it seldom or never mentions awakening and conversion. It does not reject awakening and conversion. But it is unable to find an organic place for them in connection with baptismal grace.

Other preaching speaks clearly of awakening and conversion. But it never mentions Baptism, not because it rejects the regenerative effect of Baptism, but because it is unable to provide a place for Baptism in connection with awakening and conversion.

One who is somewhat well informed will know how much of both these kinds of preaching there is in our day. And both will work harm by suppressing such important phases of the Gospel's saving truth. It will be of great importance both for preaching and for the care of souls to have placed awakening and conversion in the right relation to baptismal grace. It will be of importance both in dealing with the God-fearing child that has remained in the grace of Baptism, and with the backslider who is awakened and led to conversion.

I

The Baptismal Gift of Salvation

OUR inquiry concerns itself with the relation between regeneration in Infant Baptism on the
one hand and awakening and conversion on the
other. Naturally, then, we take as our starting-point
the baptism of the child. But before we proceed to
speak about Infant Baptism, we must very briefly
ascertain what the Scriptures tell us about Baptism
and the gift of salvation which the Lord has joined
to it.

We begin, therefore, with the Lord's words of institution (Matt. 28:19-20): "Go ye therefore, and make
disciples of all the nations, baptizing them into the
name of the Father and of the Son and of the Holy
Spirit: teaching them to observe all things whatsoever I commanded you."

These words show us, in the first place, that the
Lord here speaks of a *new* Baptism, different from
the baptism of John, with which he himself had been
baptized, and which he made use of in his early min-
istry (John 3:22 and 4:2). The baptism of John was,
he himself says, a symbolic act only, containing no
gift of salvation. "I indeed baptize you in water unto
repentance: but he that cometh after me is mightier
than I, whose shoes I am not worthy to bear. He
shall baptize you in the Holy Spirit and in fire"
(Matt. 3:11). Now after his resurrection Jesus instituted the Baptism which John had foretold, the Baptism by means of which he gives what the baptism
of John only symbolized.

Thus, too, the apostles understood this command
of Jesus. They understood the Baptism he speaks of
here as a Baptism different from the baptism of John.

This follows most clearly from the account in Acts
19:1-5. Paul meets some of the disciples of John in
Ephesus and asks them if they received the Holy
Spirit when they believed. They answer: "Nay, we
did not so much as hear that the Holy Spirit was
given." Into what then were ye baptized, asks Paul.
They reply: "Into John's baptism." And then Paul
baptized them into the name of the Lord Jesus.

In the second place, these words of Jesus show us
that Baptism is the means whereby men are made
disciples of Jesus. And by disciples of the Messiah

are meant men who are partakers in and recipients of the Messiah's gift of salvation. And John had already prophesied that the Messiah's one great gift of salvation is the Spirit. "He shall baptize you in the Holy Spirit and in fire." In the words of the Great Commission the Lord thus ordains the act of Baptism as the outward means whereby men become partakers of the Messianic salvation.

In the third place, the expression, "to baptize into the name of the Father and of the Son and of the Holy Spirit," shows that the gift of salvation which is joined to the act of Baptism is participation in the complete revelation of salvation as achieved in our world by the triune God. This means, then, that in Baptism man becomes a partaker of all the saving grace which God has put into the world.

Have we now understood these words of Jesus aright by interpreting them in this way?

We can test this most readily by ascertaining how the apostles understood the baptismal command of Jesus. They were supplied by the Lord with divine grace to understand him rightly and to interpret his utterances correctly in all points, consequently also these words of his concerning Baptism.

Let us now see how the apostles express themselves concerning the gift of salvation which is connected with the outward Baptism with water.

In this brief survey we shall not examine all the

apostolic sayings concerning Baptism; we shall consider only the most distinctive ones.

Let us notice how the New Testament authors with one accord connect the gift of the *forgiveness of sins* with Baptism. Peter speaks thus: "Repent ye, and be baptized every one of you in the name of Jesus Christ unto *the remission of your sins*" (Acts 2:38). "Arise, and be baptized, and *wash away thy sins,*" Ananias tells Paul (Acts 22:16). And in Hebrews 10:22 it says: "Let us draw near with a true heart in fulness of faith, having our *hearts sprinkled* from an evil conscience: and having our *body washed* with pure water." Here Baptism is not expressly mentioned; but that the author has Baptism in mind is perfectly apparent, because the church possessed no other act whereby the body was washed with pure water. And the author says that at the same time as the body was washed with pure water the heart was sprinkled from an evil conscience, namely through the remission of the guilt of sin.

Let us next observe how the New Testament writers *join the gift of the Holy Spirit to Baptism.* Peter says: "Be baptized every one of you in the name of Jesus Christ unto the remission of your sins; and *ye shall receive the gift of the Holy Spirit*" (Acts 2:38). And Paul says: "In one Spirit were we all baptized into one body" (1 Cor. 12:13). True enough, some have understood these words of Paul as referring to a baptism of the Spirit, having nothing in common with the Baptism with water. But the expression here does not allow such an interpretation. It says: baptized in one Spirit *into one body*. Here Paul has reference to the act of God whereby we become members of the body of Christ, and that is, of course, *regeneration*. And Paul joins regeneration to the Baptism with water; we read (Titus 3:5): "not by works done in righteousness, which we did ourselves, but according to his mercy he saved us, through *the washing of regeneration* and renewing of the Holy Spirit."

In this instance, too, some have thought that the passage does not refer to the washing of Baptism. The expression "baptism," like the expression "washing of water with the word" (Eph. 5:26), they have taken to be a figurative expression. But this is in direct opposition to all sound methods of interpretation. The churches which received these epistles had only one washing. And when the author uses this term with the definite article, *the* washing, no reader could think of anything else but the washing of Baptism. And if the author had had another washing in mind, he would have had to indicate it.

Finally, we shall notice Paul's statement that *through Baptism we become united with Christ* (Rom. 6:4-5; Col. 2:12). And if Christ was made unto us wisdom, righteousness, and redemption, as Paul says in 1 Cor. 1:30, then it is clear that Baptism, by uniting us with Christ, makes us partakers of the full salvation; so a person cannot be given more than what is given him in Baptism.

Thus we have proved, then, that our understanding of the words of institution of Jesus is right.

II

Baptism as Infant Baptism

MOST of the difficulties concerning the question of Baptism are associated with Infant Baptism. And because I take it for granted that you, my young friends, either already have contended or in the future will have to contend with these difficulties, I desire to treat of them here, in order that we may have a solid Scriptural foundation upon which to stand as we proceed to speak of regeneration in Infant Baptism. Let us deal with the arguments against Infant Baptism in the following order:

1. The history of the earliest church furnishes, it is maintained, conclusive proof that the baptizing of infants is a human ordinance, which arose long after the death of the apostles and which came about because the church already at that time was begin-

ning to grow worldly. And for that reason, also, it is contended, Infant Baptism was *enjoined* upon the whole church when the union between church and state took place in 325 A.D.

2. There is no warrant in Holy Writ for baptizing children. Not one command to baptize children can be found in all Scripture. Furthermore, it is never related in Scripture that children were baptized. True enough, it says that upon several occasions some were baptized with their whole household (Acts 16: 33; 1 Cor. 1:16). But nothing is said to indicate that there were children in these households. Of course, some Jewish families may have been childless. But even though there were children, yet there is nothing which says that they were *little* children.

3. Not only is it true that the Scriptures say nothing about the baptism of children but there are, on the contrary, passages which show clearly that children should not be baptized, it is maintained. Jesus did not baptize the little children which the mothers brought to him. He did, however, take them in his arms and lay his hands upon them and bless them (Mark 10:13-16).

4. The Scriptures name *requirements* for Baptism. "Repent ye, and be baptized every one of you," says Peter (Acts 2:38). "He that *believeth* and is baptized shall be saved," says Mark 16:6. But little children

cannot fulfill these conditions. For that reason the baptism of children should be delayed until they grow old enough to repent and believe.

5. Neither do children need Baptism in that age, some say. They have not as yet committed any sins and they are still so sweet and innocent. Furthermore, Jesus says himself that the kingdom of God belongs to them (Mark 10:14).

*

1. The earliest history of Baptism is not such a simple historical question as the opponents of Infant Baptism seem to think. The baptism of children is presupposed and spoken of by the Church Fathers very soon after the death of John the Apostle. We note that the two types of baptismal practice run parallel until about the year 250 A.D. At this time the practice which baptized both adults and children emerges victorious. This is a very difficult historical problem. Both of these opposite methods of procedure in baptizing could not have originated with the apostles. Consequently, one of them has departed from the apostolic practice. This is all the more remarkable when we think of the authority the apostles had in the churches. Which is now the original apostolic practice, and which a departure?

As an answer to these difficult questions, I shall adduce the following:

In the first place: Those Church Fathers who defend the Baptism of children emphasize explicitly that
Infant Baptism was practiced by the apostles. And
the Fathers who reject Infant Baptism never deny
this assertion. They do not attack Infant Baptism on
historical grounds, but for intellectual reasons. "Why
does the innocent age hasten to the washing of Baptism?" says Tertullian.

In the second place: When the administration of
Baptism to children was attacked, it was because of
a view of Baptism which early had crept into the
church, namely, that it was impossible for one who
had been baptized and then had fallen away from
God to be converted again. As a result of this view,
it was very common to postpone Baptism as long as
possible, even to the death-bed, in order to guard
oneself in the best possible way against falling away
after being baptized. But that makes it clear why
they did not want to baptize little children. Thus clear
light is thrown upon the struggle against Infant Baptism in earliest times.

2. Scripture does not enjoin the Baptism of children; neither does it tell of children being baptized.
That is true. But when men say that they reject Infant Baptism for this reason, they are not absolutely
truthful. In that case the same people would have to
reject other things also. Women's participation in the

Lord's Supper is nowhere commanded in the Scriptures. Neither is it related anywhere that women partook of the Sacrament of the Altar. If the opponents of Infant Baptism who thus feel themselves bound by the letter of Scripture were serious and sincere, they would also certainly be compelled to forbid women to go to the Table of the Lord.

But as far as I know, no one takes such a pedantic and unspiritual attitude as that when it pertains to the administration of the Lord's Supper. That being the case, we must have the right to ask: Why is it done when it pertains to the administration of Baptism? No, *this* is not *the reason* for rejecting the Baptism of children. It is only a *subterfuge* to which they resort for concealment.

In regard to the kernel of the matter itself, the warrant for Infant Baptism in the Scriptures, I will say: Christ has instituted neither *Adult* Baptism nor *Infant* Baptism. He has instituted *Baptism*. That is: He has once for all ordained by his creative Word what the saving effect of Baptism shall be and what gift of salvation shall accompany the act as often as it is administered. On the other hand, Jesus has not said when and where the act should be administered and who should be baptized. That he has left to his church to decide under the guidance of the Spirit of God.

Exactly the same is the case with the Lord's Sup-

per. He instituted it and ordained once for all what
gift of salvation was to accompany this act. On the
other hand, he said nothing about who should go to
the Supper.

From the baptismal command we see very clearly
that Baptism and the Word are the only means by
which men can be made disciples of Jesus. Those who
do not become disciples by these means cannot, on
the whole, become disciples.* Therefore children also
must become disciples of Jesus by these means if they,
on the whole, may as children become disciples of
Jesus.

3. But, it is argued, Jesus did not baptize the little
children which the parents brought to him. He took
them in his arms and laid his hands upon them and
blessed them. "That is what I do with my little children," a Baptist once said to me when we were dis-
cussing this. "Indeed," said I, "doing that, and doing
it often, too, certainly does not hurt your children.
But I presume you realize that Jesus has never enjoined this upon you as a means of salvation. On the
contrary, he has expressly commanded you to make
disciples of *all* by *baptizing* and teaching them."

---

*At this point the tormenting question arises for many: What becomes
of those children who die unbaptized? We must answer this the way
the ancients did: God has bound *us* to the means of grace. He himself
is *not* bound to them. He *can*, therefore, save these little children by
means unknown to us. That he *wills* it is evident from this, that it is
not his will that one of these little ones should perish (Matt. 18:14).

The reason that Jesus did not baptize the little ones, but merely took them in his arms and blessed them, is exceedingly simple. It was because he had not as yet instituted Christian Baptism in the name of the triune God. Therefore he did not baptize adults, either, who came to him.

4. But do children need the gift of Baptism?

Here, assuredly, we touch upon the fundamental difficulty in the question of Baptism. Here is where intellectual doubt concerning Infant Baptism generally originates. Children are so sweet and innocent. And of course they have not, as yet, been able to *commit* any sin. And then, too, Scripture says that they belong to the kingdom of God.

No, Scripture does not say that. The statement of Jesus in Mark 10:14 does not say that by any means. He says that the kingdom of God belongs to them! not that the little ones belong to the kingdom of God. The disciples of Jesus thought that the kingdom of God was not intended for little children. Therefore they sought to prevent the parents from occupying Jesus' time with these little ones. Then Jesus became angry and said that the kingdom of God is intended for them.

"Is this a correct interpretation of these words of Jesus?" some ask. Yes, it is. That Jesus with these words never did want to say that children by virtue

of their natural birth belong to the kingdom of God,
every one should know who has read Jesus' words
to Nicodemus: "That which is born of the flesh is
flesh" (John 3:6). Therefore every individual, also
little children, must be born anew in order to enter
into the kingdom of God.

We find the same thought also in Paul's writings
(Eph. 2:3): "We are all by nature children of wrath."
"By nature"—that means: Our condition at birth is
such that we are subject to the wrath of God which
rests upon our whole fallen race. It is correct enough
to say: "The infant has not, as yet, *committed* any
sin." But we cannot be born into this sinful race without bearing our share of the race's guilt.

5. But are children capable of receiving the gift of
Baptism?

Scripture names repentance and faith as the conditions upon which Baptism can have any saving effect upon the one who is baptized. But a child certainly cannot repent and believe. Therefore Baptism
must be postponed until the child is old enough to
be able to repent and believe.

So they say, and so they do. And, of course, it appears logically unassailable. There is only this little
hitch in it: the plain words of Jesus are diametrically
opposed to it. The ordinance of Jesus has been turned
upside down completely. He says that we adults must

repent and *become as little children* in order to enter
into the kingdom of God (Matt. 18:3). Furthermore,
he even says that whosoever shall not receive the kingdom of God as a little child shall in no wise enter
therein (Mark 10:15). But the opponents of Infant
Baptism say that the children must become like us
adults; then they, too, will be permitted to enter into
the kingdom of God.

A few still argue: "Yes, but were the children to
which Jesus had reference *so* small that they could
not repent and believe?" The answer to this objection
is: The record says that they *brought (carried)* them
to Jesus. They were at least that small. And the Greek
expression in Luke 18:15, *brephos,* really means fetus
and is used in that sense, for instance, in Luke 1:41.
But it is also used of infants and very small children.

Thus it has become clear to us that Jesus looks upon
children, not only as being capable of receiving the
gift of the kingdom of God, but so receptive, even,
that they are examples of receptivity for us adults.

*

The view of Baptism and of the child which rejects
Infant Baptism is very deeply rooted. It is not merely a misunderstanding of Baptism and of the child;
it goes much deeper than that. Fundamentally it is
a misunderstanding of the very truth concerning *sin
and grace.*

The opponents of Infant Baptism have not been able to hold fast to the statements of Scripture regarding man's total moral impotence as a result of the fall in sin. It comes to light most clearly in their preaching of repentance. It is preached thus: "Man must by repentance tear himself loose from his former sins and cease to love sin." If the sinner is not able to accomplish this, the surrender is not a wholehearted one, it is said.

Their preaching of faith shows the same thing. Man, by his faith, must draw grace unto himself. Grace is, indeed, free. That is, he who seeks it can get it. Faith is the hand by means of which the sinner reaches out for and appropriates grace.

If repentance and faith are understood in this way, it is clear that the little child can have neither of them. The child cannot put forth any of the soul-exertion which, according to this conception, is absolutely necessary in order that the grace of God may be transferred to the heart of the sinner.

In Scripture this is presented in an entirely different light.

Man is lost because of sin. He possesses no power to tear himself loose from his old sins, still less to cease loving sin. Scripture tells us, moreover, that Christ came to release the *captives*. It tells us, likewise, that the mind of the flesh is enmity against God, and "that which is born of the flesh is flesh" until it is born of God.

Repentance, therefore, does not consist in this, that man is able by the power of his own will to tear himself loose from his former sins; neither in this, that man is able to compel himself to hate sin and to love God. No, repentance consists in this, that the sinner, convicted by the Holy Spirit of his sins, submits to this conviction and confesses that he is bound by the chains of sin and that he loves sin and not God.

Faith is not a soul-exertion or a condition of the soul which makes us worthy to receive the grace of God. Neither is it a power by means of which we should draw unto ourselves the grace of God.

That is not necessary, because grace is free. Not only in the sense that all may *seek* it. It is as free as the air which envelopes us on every hand and forces itself in upon us as soon as it secures the least access. Such is the grace of God in Christ.

The propitiation which Christ made by his life and death he made as the representative of and the substitute for the race. Therefore this propitiation is the property of the race. The covenant which God made in the death of Christ consists in this, that he takes upon himself to impart to each member of the race the salvation which through Christ belongs to the race. See 2 Cor. 5:18-19, where Paul mentions "the word of "reconciliation" as a part of the dispensation

of salvation which God perfected in and by the death
of Christ.

As a consequence of this covenant, God provides
that grace searches for the individual sinner. It is not
the sinner, therefore, who first seeks grace. No, grace
has already found the sinner the moment the sinner
begins to seek grace.

Because grace searches for the sinner long before
the sinner thinks of grace, Baptism becomes Infant
Baptism. Grace searches for man as soon as he is born.
The little child *shall,* according to God's covenant, receive its part of the finished salvation, which it has
a right to because it is born into the race which Jesus
has redeemed. The child *can* receive a part in this
salvation, Jesus says. It is to that extent receptive that
it is an example for us adults in receiving the kingdom of God.

How, then, does the child receive the kingdom of
God?

It, of course, has no idea of what is taking place
in the moment of Baptism. It cannot think, consequently neither repent nor believe as we adults do.
But it can do something that we adults first learn
through repentance and faith: It remains passive, not
opposing the grace of God. Jesus gains unimpeded
access to this little human life with all his grace and
gifts.

Now Jesus tells us adults that if we do not receive

the kingdom of God "as a little child," we shall never enter therein. But how shall we adults get to the point where we, as the child, become submissive and do not hinder Jesus from entering with all his salvation? Of a truth, says Jesus, *through repentance* we become as children (Matt. 18:3).

Here we see, consequently, what purpose repentance should serve us adults. It is to remove the opposition by means of which we have prevented Jesus from coming to us with all his grace. Repentance and faith in the adult consist, therefore, simply in this, that the adult realizes and acknowledges his helplessness and decides to surrender himself unconditionally to the Savior. For Jesus needs *help* neither from the little child nor from the adult. All he needs is *access*.

Thus we have seen that administration of Baptism as Infant Baptism is precisely an expression of how free and unmerited is the grace of God.

This throws light upon the peculiar historical fact, that it is the *Reformed* Church which has had difficulties with Infant Baptism. The Lutheran Church has had no difficulties, except such as have been injected into it from the Reformed Church through the influence of individuals here and there. That the Lutheran Church has, without difficulty, retained Baptism as Infant Baptism is precisely because it has had such a clear view of human depravity and the unmerited gift of God's salvation.

III

The Unconscious Life

AFTER this exposition of the baptismal gift of salvation and the applicability of Baptism to children, we now turn to the question of *the effect of Baptism in the child*.

Theoretically, the question can be answered plainly enough. Through Baptism the child is grafted into a living connection with Christ and receives thereby a part in the full salvation: forgiveness of sins, sonship, and the new life through the Holy Spirit. But it is more difficult to give a *practical* reply to this question. What is it that takes place within the child in the moment of Baptism?

What is done *to* the child is not so difficult to determine, because that is precisely the same as what is done to the adult who is baptized. The child is delivered from its guilt by becoming a partaker in the atonement of Jesus Christ. Thereby it is raised to the estate of sonship.

What is done within the child is, on the contrary, more difficult to determine. True enough, we can forthwith determine this as follows: The Holy Spirit accomplishes regeneration in the little one. But if we ask: What occurs in the child, what is it that psychologically has taken place in this little life, we straightway realize the difficulty.

Then, too, it is a question whether we are not at this point approaching the mysterious realm into which the human mind cannot tread and where we simply in holy awe should take off our shoes. We know, of course, that regeneration both with adults and infants is the great life mystery, which no human mind is able to think through or explain. As we proceed to our investigation of this matter, we do not intend to undertake anything so unreasonable as to explain the inexplicable. But we do wish to consider everything that we *can* understand, and analyze it as far as we are able.

*

When we set out to investigate the effect of Baptism in the infant, we encounter the difficulty that the child has only *unconscious life*. For we are as yet little acquainted with the nature and the laws of this

life. But we shall now try to gather the knowledge
we have of the unconscious life and thereby elucidate
the relation between the unconscious and the conscious life.

In the first place, then, we shall record the simple
truth that every normally developed human life consists of these two kinds of life, the conscious and the
unconscious. And the relation between these we may
express by a mathematical figure, thus: They are to
each other as two concentric circles, two circles with
the same center but of different sizes. The *greater* of
these circles is the unconscious life. It may possibly be
that many will be surprised on hearing this. It is also
in itself remarkable that the life of a human being,
which is, of course, a personal life, really moves more
in the realm of the unconscious than in that of the
conscious. But it is not difficult to show that this is
actually so.

In the first place, we lived at least two years in the
unconscious life before the conscious life began to
awaken. Most people lose consciousness some time before the unconscious life is extinguished in death. With
some this may take several minutes; with others, several hours, days, or weeks.

In the second place, we may refer to sleep. Sleep
temporarily renders our conscious life extinct, so that
only the unconscious functions. It is highly remarkable that we spend such a large part of our brief life-

time in sleep. When we take into account that the child sleeps so much during the first two years and that the same usually repeats itself in old age, we can no doubt say that every human being sleeps away on an average one third of his lifetime.

In the third place, we can make reference to the fact that also in the awakened state we experience vastly more than the little we apprehend in our consciousness to such an extent that we can say to ourselves, "Now I experienced it." Thus we see every moment much more than we are conscious of having seen or, as we say, "paid attention to." Likewise our ears catch many more sounds every moment than we take notice of. In the midst of the most alert state, our thoughts take a vacation—as, for instance, during meetings. We discover suddenly that we have been absent in the spirit for a while. Reference can be made likewise to the purely automatic organic functions within the body, digestion, for instance. We sit at the table and eat and do not for a moment think of how we masticate or how we digest our food. Furthermore, digestion is best accomplished when we do not think of it. Those people who begin to worry too much about their digestion generally develop indigestion.

Just this little investigation reveals to us that we all, every moment of our life, experience much more than we can consciously grasp and hold up before ourselves and account for. My conscious life is, therefore, only a small portion of the life which I live every moment.

*

The unconscious life-circle is, meanwhile, not only the greater. It is also first. Our conscious life begins at the age of two to grow forth out of the unconscious. This tells us a little about the dependency of the conscious life upon the unconscious. The unconscious is, so to speak, the root from which the conscious grows, to which it is connected all the way, and upon which it must forever depend for support.

This is elucidated exceptionally well by sleep. The conscious life is to such a degree dependent upon the unconscious that we must spend almost a third part of every twenty-four hours in the unconscious state. That is, the conscious life must at regular intervals immerse itself into the depths of the unconscious life. Therefrom it returns new and fresh, as our bodies do after a bath.

How dependent our conscious life is upon the unconscious is brought out still more clearly by the fact that sleep strengthens us most when it is deep, that is, when it has rendered the conscious life completely extinct. As long as we are sunk in torpor and receive semiconscious impressions from without and work them over in our dreams, so long do we not sleep and rest really well.

The dependency of the conscious life upon the unconscious we see most clearly from the fact that the conscious life simply cannot exist without receiving sufficient and regular sleep. In fact, we see that people who for one reason or another do not receive enough sleep for a long period of time, lose the ability to live the conscious life and enter into the darkness of insanity.

The unconscious part of our life is now termed *subconsciousness*. It has to an exceptional degree attracted to itself the attention of our day and is studied energetically and thoroughly by present-day students of psychology. There is scarcely a subject being studied with such interest in our time as the subconscious life.

We Christians should be especially thankful for this study. It will assuredly throw light upon many phases of Christian soul-life, and precisely on the most obscure phases of the Christian's soul-life, namely, those which are not directly subject to the control of consciousness and will. Above all, this study will certainly help us to understand more easily the soul-life of the child, which moves to such an essential degree in the subconscious right up to the moment when it is grown and fully developed. We can without doubt say that the conscious life of the child is in the process of awakening all the way from the age of two up through all the years of childhood until it is fully grown. The real dividing line between child and adult is, therefore, this, that the conscious life of the adult has attained its normal relationship to the subconscious.

*

Our life with God also consists of *two circles,* the conscious and the unconscious. Here, too, the unconscious is the *greater.* Our life with God includes every moment much more than we can perceive with our minds and comprehend in our emotions.

Life with God is an organism which functions uninterruptedly as long as a person possesses this life. It functions unceasingly also when the conscious life is not functioning, thus *during sleep,* and when the conscious life is occupied with other things than thinking of the God-life, for instance *during work.*

It is essential for us to be clear upon this phase of the God-life. It will free us from much unnecessary fear and inward unrest, and it will give our God-life the inward rest and balance which it needs in order to grow.

Especially in the first period of his Christian life, we are inclined to think that life with God consists only in the *thoughts* we have about God together with the *emotions* which attend these thoughts. For that reason we are during this period so afraid of all that leads us away from thinking about God. It is even easy to fear and shun work since it hinders us from thinking about God.

Now this leads to an unnatural and forced God-life, a trait which we find also in older Christians within those Christian groups which have little or no vision of the unconscious side of the Christian life. They are especially tempted to force, by artificial means, the emotional life of the Christian up to an unnatural height.

If, on the other hand, we can come to see that the God-life is a life which lives and grows uninterruptedly, also when cognition, feeling, and will are otherwise occupied, then we will get the natural rest and repose in our soul-life which is so indispensable to the sound growth of the God-life. Then we will go to our daily work with joy and gratitude, even if it prevents us from thinking unceasingly about God. We will gradually learn to thank God especially for work because it is such a natural and simple means of keeping our hearts and our thoughts from sinning.

Many believers complain that they have so much to do that it is difficult for them to care for their life in God. For me the opposite is the case. My vacations are as a rule the weakest seasons for my spiritual life. Never is the temptation to rest from the battle against

my sins greater. My spiritual life fares best when I
am at my regular work.

Jesus expressed himself once on this unconscious
side of the God-life: "So is the kingdom of God, as
if a man should cast seed upon the earth; and should
sleep and rise night and day, and the seed should
spring up and grow, *he knoweth not how*. The earth
beareth fruit *of herself;* first the blade, then the ear,
then the full grain in the ear" (Mark 4:26-28).

Of herself the earth beareth fruit, Jesus says. Of itself life in God grows, and not because I think about
it. With my will I am only to give it place in my
thoughts and provide it with the nourishment which
it needs and which I can provide for it through the
means of grace.

In this connection I shall mention a condition which
is one of the most painful here in our world. I
am thinking of the believers who become insane. Of
course, in and of itself this is a grievous matter. But
what often becomes the hardest for those concerned
is that the insane one behaves in such a way that they
must believe he has fallen away from God. Thus these
who before becoming insane were warm-hearted believers often begin to curse or speak wantonly and
unchastely. Or, as is often seen in the case of old
people, when hardening of the arteries goes to the
brain, they may become so ugly and contrary, even
malicious, that those near to them must believe that

they have fallen away from God in their old age. The worst phase appears when these insane people commit suicide. Many people think that no hope remains because suicide leads directly to eternal perdition.

This conception rests, meanwhile, upon a complete misunderstanding of insanity. It is not recognized that the insane one is not responsible for his words and acts because he has lost the control over his life which consciousness and will exercise. Then the evil which is in every human soul gains unhindered permission to find expression in word and in deed.

Even before becoming insane, the one concerned carried within him all this hideousness and wickedness. But then it was subjugated daily and kept under control by the holy consciousness and will of the new man.

In this connection it is of great value to know the relation between the conscious and the unconscious life. We saw above that the God-life lives its life uninterruptedly also when the conscious life is rendered extinct, during sleep, for instance. Thus the God-life remains uninjured and continues to live also when the believer's conscious life is extinguished by insanity. A believer, therefore, who becomes insane is not more responsible for what he does then than he is responsible for what he does and says in sleep.

As comfort and consolation to those whose believ-

ing relatives or friends become insane, still another
thing may be mentioned. Just as impossible as it is
for a believer to fall away from God while sleeping,
so impossible is it for a believer to fall away from
God as long as he is insane. The believers who become incurably insane are, therefore, already eternal-
ly saved and forever beyond all danger of falling away.

This is the comforting ray of light which gives
solace in the midst of insanity's terrible darkness.

It should be superfluous, but permit me, nevertheless, for safety's sake, to remind you that I wish by no
means to defend suicide with these thoughts. What
I have said here does not apply to all who take their
own life, but to the insane only. Not, furthermore,
to all insane people either, but only to such insane
people as were believers when they went insane.

*

Also in the life with God the unconscious life is
the first to function. God brings about by supernatural means a living connection with the unconscious
part of our person. Before the conscious life of the
child awakens, God touches its unconscious life with
his lifegiving Spirit. He takes our life's finest and
deepest roots and plants them into God's own life-
ground, so our unconscious life from that moment receives nourishment and the impetus of life from God
himself.

And that is what happens to the infant *in Baptism*.
The little slip of humanity is thereby put into living relationship with God. It receives life with God.
Jesus illustrated this living relationship on one occasion in the beautiful parable of the vine and the
branches. It is through Baptism that the little one is
grafted into Christ. And no matter how small the
branch may be, it has, nevertheless, the same life as
the trunk.

At the first birth the child was brought into living relationship with the whole sinful race and thereby with the author and captain of sin, the devil. The
child is not conscious of this living connection, which
is, nevertheless, just as real and just as active. The
child's early personal life is filled with and molded
by this sinful life content.

It is this inherited sinful life that God meets by
regenerating the child, that is, giving it relationship
with a life of an entirely different kind, with the good
life, with God's own life. The evil life is not to be
permitted to work alone in the child. Now the little
one receives, because it is a member of the race which
Christ has redeemed, in the moment of rebirth, its
part of the salvation which, according to the covenant
of God, is given to and transferred into every human
being which does not refuse to accept his portion of
salvation.

The child *cannot* as yet deny the grace of God access. Therefore God can, *unhindered,* give the infant a part in the finished salvation. Through Baptism the child is grafted into Christ, and thus it gains access to receive the full salvation which is included in the person of Christ. But for the time being it can neither apply nor make use of all the life and vitality with which it has become connected. The living relationship takes place, for the time being, only in the unconscious life. For the child has as yet only this life.

*

Now, if we are to get any idea of what is taking place during this time in the soul-life of the child, we must observe that the unconscious part of our person is in constant and lively association with every environment which partakes of this form of life— namely, with God, with angels, with devils, and with human beings.

The unconscious part of our life constitutes the natural root-connection with the all-life. Through our subconsciousness the bottomless and endless ocean of life which surrounds us on all sides washes into our person and fills and molds it with its impressions and subconscious life-promptings.

The conscious part of our life is like an island which shoots up out of the endless ocean of life. We could also express it in this way: It is that part of life which is our *peculiar possession*. The unconscious part of our life, on the other hand, is a part of the great ocean of life over which we have no personal control, either with our mind or will.

Along what paths and according to what laws the life-currents move in the great ocean of life with which we communicate through subconsciousness, we are not qualified to trace, at least not at the present time. The laws governing the subconscious life are being studied energetically today. And it is possible that they will gradually come to be known somewhat better.

But for the time being we can only point out that our souls *are* in a peculiar subconscious life-communication of this kind, without being able to show further *how* this takes place. We see before our eyes every day that this hidden communication unites souls and fills them with a peculiar common life, which can only be explained by means of subconsciousness. We see how larger or smaller groups of people in this way can be filled with the same moods and emotions, the same thoughts and fantasies, and the same plans and purposes.

Let us only think of what we call "the family spirit," "the national soul," "the spirit of the times," and "public opinion."

To illustrate this I shall cite the following two examples.

When World War I broke out in 1914, we saw in a characteristic way how the German national soul awakened and set the whole nation in motion. Let us first look at the common *conceptions* which immediately filled great and small souls in the whole German Empire: the German people were surrounded by enemies who begrudged them their ability and power, and who now planned to crush a disagreeable competitor. Let us next observe the common *feelings* which surged through this richly emotional nation of millions: devotion to Kaiser and people, enthusiasm for the German people's God-given task as the world-ruling nation. Let us finally notice the common *volitional* life which was instantaneously set in motion in those days, from the aged and down to the little children: a willingness to sacrifice, so imposingly great that it has in all likelihood scarcely an equal in history.

In a community in Norway a horrible murder was committed. A young girl was murdered in broad daylight only a stone's throw away from a much-traveled highway. Her body was mutilated in a most terrible manner. Naturally, a most diligent search for the murderer was made, but he was never found. There was something inexplicable and mysterious about it all. Meanwhile, shortly afterward, the family of the murdered girl pointed out a man in the neighborhood as the murderer. The whole community seized the thought at once, and without further ado called him

the murderer on every occasion when during that
time they discussed the murder. The police made an
investigation in the case, but found no cause for the
accusation. The man himself took the matter in a
humorous way and called himself the murderer, and
even came to the postoffice and asked if there was
any mail for the murderer. But to this day the whole
community is convinced that he is the murderer.

Thus the folk-soul works. Without possessing legal
proof, the family centers its suspicions upon one certain man. And this unfounded suspicion and antipa-
thy spreads like lightning through the whole community.

*

We all have a tendency to value too highly the conscious part of our life. It is, of course, true enough
that self-consciousness is the essential elements in the
life which we call *personal*. No life is personal without self-consciousness.

Thus also in our relation to God. No adult can
become a child of God but through the workings of
God upon his unconscious life. The divine influence
which leads to repentance must reach up into the conscious life of the individual. For conversion is impossible except by a conscious and free choice.

We easily value the conscious life too highly, nevertheless. We believe that consciousness is the only portal

into personality's sanctuary: the conscience and the will. We overlook the organic continuity which exists between the conscious and the unconscious life in our person.

Subconsciousness may be likened to a *repository* where all thoughts, ideas, moods, and emotions are preserved so absolutely intact that not a single impression which has passed through either our conscious or only our unconscious life disappears. Here all of our experiences in life lie safely stored.

This remarkable fact has been verified in different ways, partly by dream-life and partly by the so-called cleavages of consciousness. Due to an injury to the brain or to some other shock, a person suddenly forgets himself, literally speaking. He does not remember his name, does not remember the past, cannot speak his old language, or eat, or walk, etc. He must learn this all over again, just like a little child. But then it happens occasionally that a person like this suddenly begins to speak fluently a language which he could not speak before the shock. Investigation reveals that the person involved had spoken this language as a little child but had forgotten it again completely, just as children quickly forget a language when they no longer hear or speak it. Thus it comes to light that subconsciousness had preserved this knowledge of the language in question safely and faithfully although the conscious life had long since forgotten it, yes, not even remembered that it had spoken this language.

Subconsciousness is, meanwhile, not only a repository which preserves a dead mass of psychological impressions. It is much more a *workshop,* which works over all of the accumulated material according to laws which we cannot define more closely.

We experience only that subconsciousness does a quiet and unnoticed work of this kind, the result of which it sends up some fine day from its subterranean workshop into the clear daylight of consciousness.

Thus most of us remember how we sat evenings in childhood working at a difficult problem in arithmetic and finally had to go to bed without having solved it. Then we went at it again the next morning, and then we solved it very easily perhaps. For the subconscious mind had had time to work over the accumulated impressions, and now it sent the solution at once up into our conscious thinking.

We who preach the Word of God often have the experience that a text gives us great difficulty. It is impossible for us to find a line of thought leading into the text and opening it for us. We sit for hours, perhaps, working on our discourse, but with no results. Finally we are compelled to leave our work, downcast and dejected. A day or two later we attack the same text, likely with a great deal of determination. And then, we often have the experience that the text

opens itself and we see with our inner eye our whole
sermon; it is a joy and a pleasure to work it out. Just
such service subconsciousness is willing to perform.
We should, therefore, see to it that it gets the time
and the opportunity to do this work for us, whether
it be problems in arithmetic or sermons or other things.

The common sense of the people has long since discovered this fact, long before any research worker had
discovered its psychological foundation and consistency.
Experienced and sober people never acquiesce very
easily and quickly to a new plan which is proposed
to them. On such occasions they reply: "I'll have to
sleep on it." Experience tells them, that they will be
able to pass judgment more clearly in the matter
when they have slept on it. Then the subconsciousness gets time to consider the matter from all angles.

*

It is not difficult to see that a knowledge of this
subconscious life will be of the greatest importance
both for our *judgment* and in our *treatment* of the
child.

In the first place, the child communicates with its
environment long before it is at all conscious of it.
Through the subconsciousness it gathers from its very
birth, yes, even before birth, impressions of which the
subconsciousness never lets go but retains and assimilates.

In the second place, the conscious life of the child grows out of the subconscious. The subconscious life's store of impressions gives the conscious life its fundamental control and marks the course of the child's later personal life.

In the third place, this should give us much confidence in our association with and our treatment of both children and adults. The good and the sacred impressions we are in position to give them they will never lose, even though they were not conscious of the impressions they received. By filling their subconsciousness with sacred impressions we are permitted to have a part in forming their later personal life.

This will also give us a great deal of confidence in associating with adults, especially in our relation to the unsaved. We pray for them and we speak with them now and then about the one thing needful. But we understand that our exhortations so easily tire them and harden them. We see how they live their worldly life thoughtlessly and indifferently. This knowledge may make us discouraged and despondent.

Then it is well to know the subconscious life and realize that all the impressions we leave with them, both the conscious and the unconscious, through our actions, our words, our being, and our spirit, are all accumulated in the subconsciousness, and not one is lost. And while they live their conscious life thoughtlessly and frivolously, their subconsciousness is working quietly but surely with the impressions received. Some fine day it will send the result up into the conscious life in the form of a thought of God which will have such peculiar power that it will concentrate the whole soul-life about itself. Then we say that the person concerned is *awakened*. Here we have the antecedent psychological history of awakening, how it is quietly prepared day by day down in the depths of the soul, even though neither we nor the person himself can, for the time being, see or notice it.

I do not desire in any way by this psychological explanation of awakening to obscure or weaken the work of the Spirit in a person's awakening. I only wish to point out *where* the Spirit works. During the whole preparation of the awakening he works in man's subconsciousness in a way that we cannot trace definitely. We know only from Scripture that he has access to work within the subconscious life. It is told of John the Baptist that he was filled with the Holy Spirit even from his mother's womb (Luke 1:15).

This quiet working of the Spirit which leads to the awakening in man's subconsciousness does not, meanwhile, do away with his free choice. The work of the Spirit in the subconsciousness certainly no man can withstand. He has reserved unto himself the right to do this without asking man for permission. But this work of the Spirit in the adult will never lead to *repentance* and salvation unless it extends from the subconsciousness up into the life consciously controlled by the will. Here it is that man's choice comes in. Here man determines either to make room for what the Spirit has accomplished and now consciously convicts him, or that he will employ his consciousness and his will to reject this work of the Spirit.

Sudden conversions are spoken of. That there are such is absolutely true. There are people who may have lived in a worldly, even ungodly, way for years. But they are suddenly awakened out of this condition, either at a meeting or through some other experience. They make their decision and allow themselves to be saved on the spot.

But in reality this did not come to pass as suddenly as it would seem. It appeared that way only in the consciousness of the one concerned. He did not recognize the quiet work which the Spirit had done during all these years in his subconscious life.

This circumstance gives us confidence when we pray and prepare for revivals. We are to rejoice in the fact that the Spirit works quietly in people's subconsciousness. We are to be permitted to follow the Spirit in this work in man's subconscious life. That, indeed, is the great secret of *intercessory prayer*. By means of intercession we accompany the Spirit into the secret depths of the souls and influence them, although they do not for the time being surmise it.

IV

Baptism and the Word

FOLLOWING this investigation both of what Baptism is and of the child's psychological nature, we now turn to an inquiry into the relation between the grace which God has given the child in Baptism and the grace which he desires to impart to it through the other means of grace, the Word especially.

For the sake of a general view, we shall first examine this relation in the unconscious period of the child's life, and next in the conscious period of the child's life, and thereupon in the transition years, when the child passes from childhood to the adult age. And, finally, we shall inquire into the relation between the effect of Baptism and of the Word in such as have fallen away from their baptismal grace but are again awakened and converted.

A. In the Unconscious Period

In this period of the child's life we can, of course, speak of the influence of the Word upon the child in a figurative sense only. For the child lives as yet only the unconscious life. But I hold, nevertheless, that it is in order to say a little about this also as far as the unconscious child is concerned. For the little baptized child is to be met, also during this period, with the grace of God as he has ordained it through the other means of grace, even though this influence as yet is only in part and imperfect because of the stage of development in which the child is. As a matter of fact, the child should be surrounded on every side by the grace of God from the very moment of Baptism in order that its whole life from the very first may be formed by and filled with the saving grace of God.

From the moment of Baptism, the little one is a child of God. At that time it entered into a vital union with Christ and became a member of his body. Thereby the child has already become a member of the *communion of saints*. That the branch may be small means nothing in this connection; it is, nevertheless, in vital union with all the other branches on the trunk.

If we thought a little more about this, we would certainly deal differently with the little ones, not only our own little ones, but also other people's. Now we

scarcely notice them when we visit in the homes. But
if we looked upon them as members of the communion of saints, we would sacrifice both time and
interest for them and do a little for them; if nothing
else, we should pray for them.

Now, it is the Lord's will that these little ones
should benefit by the communion of saints from the
very first moment they are received into it through
Baptism. The little child is to lay hold on unconscious impressions from God *through us*. We are to
influence and by all the means we possess get in touch
with the child in this stage of its development. These
means are not so few.

In the first place, we are to influence the child
through our *prayers*. I have spoken of this before,
and so I shall not dwell upon it in detail here. I shall
only remark that this is the means by which we can
influence the child even before it is born, and, at the
same time, the means by which we at all times may
have the strongest grip on the inner life of the child.

In the next place, we influence the child through
our *spirit*. We do not think about this very often. We
think more about our words and our example. These
do influence the child tremendously, certainly much
more than we believe, and much more than the child
itself has any idea of. But stronger than all our words
and all our deeds is our spirit, that is, the *life itself
within us,* the life from which our words and our

actions spring forth like little shoots. A person's spirit always influences his surroundings, even when not a word is spoken and not a deed done.

We should note that as John the Baptist in a supernatural way was filled with the Spirit of God *even from his mother's womb,* so our children are filled with our spirit. Our spirit is, therefore, the decisive factor in the life of the child through all the years of childhood, but especially during the years in which we can reach it only through its unconscious life.

Here is the profound responsibility which devolves upon us who are parents or brothers or sisters, or who deal with little children in some other capacity. It is not sufficient that our actions are such that they furnish a good example for the child. It is not enough that our words are good and true, so that they fill the little souls with holy content. Our spirit is still more essential. We must lay the chief emphasis upon having it sanctified if we are not to harm or entirely destroy the soul-life of our children from the very first.

Most parents have no idea of how they harm their children by their untruthful, unclean, worldly, vain, and selfish spirit, injuring their children during the decisive years when the conscious life is being fashioned. I shall not make mention here of the parents who in their desire for pleasure leave their children and scarcely see them during these first years, but concentrate on social activities and leave their children

with servants who fill the little souls with their frivolous, unclean, and hypocritical spirit.

On the other hand, there are many parents who
benefit their children more than they imagine by so
living that the little ones are privileged to breathe
the clear and holy atmosphere of a God-fearing home
from the very first moment. That means something
else and more than to provide them with fine clothes,
many toys, a comfortable home, and, finally, a large
inheritance. Remember this, you who are a father or
a mother, or are to become one.

*

The child is, then, to meet something of the divine
in its parents, and that from the very first moment.

Now there is repeated in the child's life what we
see in the history of Israel. The first thing God could
reveal to this childlike people was his will, his holy
law. God's holy will is the first thing of which the
little child also can get an impression.

The child is to meet the will of God first in the
moral will of its parents, that is, through their *discipline*. Many parents are not mindful of this. Their
discipline therefore, becomes exceedingly casual and
is most generally designed to prevent the child from
doing something which is displeasing to the parents
for the moment.

This little child has the sinful natural life within

itself. It is now the parents' task through discipline to
meet and to counteract the selfishness and obstinacy
in the little one. For the impressions which now begin to enter the subconsciousness of the child are the
very ones which are to contribute to the formation
of its later personal life.

The obstinacy in the child crops out immediately.
It cries until it gets its own way. If it does not get
its own way immediately, it cries still more. If it is
humored now, it will take into its subconsciousness
the abiding and decisive impression that nothing more
is necessary in order to get its own way than to cry.

It is this subconscious stubbornness in the little one
that the parents are to meet with their discipline.
"But," many parents ask, "how can the little one be
disciplined as long as it does not understand a word
or a gesture from us?" Indeed, that is simple enough.
The discipline must be directed toward the subconsciousness of the little one, and the child will very
quickly perceive the purpose of the discipline. Let it
cry as long as it pleases. Do not humor it in its whims
and fancies. Then you will see that the child's subconsciousness soon gives it the information that it is useless to cry. If the child has had the experience of crying, for instance, three nights in succession until it
has finished, without being picked up and carried and
lulled, it will sleep the fourth night and all the suc-
ceeding nights in peace, without causing any com-

motion. Thus the child will be spared all that terrible
crying and the parents all the night vigils and the
other wear and tear involved in running to the assistance of the little tyrant every time it pleases him
to cry.

"But," says the tender mother, "what if the little
one should be crying because it is sick!" Of course,
an examination is necessary in such a case. And that
is not so difficult either. If the child is fed and cared
for at the right time; if it is warm and dry; and if
its appetite is good and its temperature normal, it
can safely be allowed to cry until it ceases of its own
accord. Its little life will then soon enter upon good
habits. It will sleep, eat, croon, and chuckle, and play
a little with its fingers until it goes to sleep again.

This bringing up of the child even in infancy is
the child's first meeting with the will of God. Through
this determined and purposeful parental discipline the
child meets for the first time the unrelenting, absolute
will, which it is useless to oppose. This is the only
impression of the sovereignty of God the child can
receive at this age. But then, too, it can receive a
strong impression of this if the parents enforce this
discipline.

This discipline should continue through childhood,
only it must be extended and enforced by more means
and methods, according as the conscious life of the
child develops. The essential elements in all discipline

is just this, that the child throughout its whole childhood meets father's and mother's moral will as an
inflexible one which can be moved neither by crying
nor by parleying and begging. Therefore, the *obedience* of the child is the sure sign whether the bringing up has been rightly undertaken. The child should
be accustomed to obey father's and mother's words
immediately and *without raising objections*. For that
reason, do *not* give *many rules* for the child's daily
life. But you must be consistent and patient enough
to demand obedience to the rules that you do give.

Such discipline during the infancy of the child will
be of decisive importance for the whole future life of
the child.

In the first place: For the child which has from the
very first met the absolute and holy will which it has
been futile to oppose; for the child which from the
very beginning has had the impression stamped upon
its subconsciousness that its own will must yield, it
will be much easier all the way later on to submit to
the discipline of its parents. The discipline will, therefore, be less painful both for the child and for the
parents.

In the second place: It will be so much easier for
this child to submit its will to that of its brothers and
sisters and other children. Its childhood will, therefore, be much easier and much more pleasant.

In the third place: It will also be easier for this child

to find its place in society at large and to submit to
the law of the land. Those children, on the other hand,
who have been able to get their own way by crying
whenever they took a notion or a fancy, have actually
been reared by their sentimental parents for a career
in crime. Look, for instance, at the little three-year-
old who in anger throws himself to the ground and
spits at his own mother and kicks and strikes in all
directions. Do you not see the criminal in the little
one? The only thing he lacks is strength to carry out
what he in his brutal and uncontrolled mind wishes.
When this child's obstinacy has been humored ten or
twelve years more, and his stubbornness and physical
powers have increased manifold, he will be fairly well
trained for a career in crime.

In the fourth place: The child that has learned from
its very infancy to bend its own will in submission
to the will of God in the discipline of its parents has
thereby gained a great advantage in its relation to
God. It will be easier for it to be kept in the baptismal life with God. For it will be easier for it to
subject its will to the will of God. And should it
fall away from God, it will most certainly be easier
for it to repent again. The most difficult thing in
repentance is to surrender one's will fully in subjection
to God's will. And this child has had regular training in doing this from its very infancy, both subcon-
sciously and consciously.

B. *In the Conscious Period of Childhood*

The great commission of Jesus commands us to make disciples of all by *baptizing* them and *teaching* them to keep all things whatsoever he commanded.

The *Word* as a means of grace is, therefore, to step in and do its work together with the grace of *Baptism*. As soon as we can make ourselves at all understood to the little ones by talking to them, we should begin to speak to them about Jesus. Many, however, postpone this because they think it is useless to speak to the child about these high and holy things before the child is old enough to "understand" them.

This is due to a misunderstanding of the child's nature. The child's strength, as long as it is a child, does not lie in "understanding" the reality it experiences, that is, thinking it over and finding the logical or rational relation between its experiences. On the contrary, the child's strength lies in receiving strong and vital impressions of everything it sees and hears. Feeling and imagination are most strongly developed in the child. And by means of these it receives and assimilates far more impressions of reality than we adults generally think, because our attitude toward the reality we experience is essentially reflective and cognitive and not intuitive and unreflective like the child's.

As a result of this, the child grasps much more than it "understands" of what we tell it about Jesus, granted that it is told in a somewhat childlike way, that is, in words and expressions that the child is accustomed to hearing and using, and in a descriptive and graphic way, so that the child's imagination is stirred and everything is portrayed before the inner eye of the child.

*

With regard to *the relation between the Word and Baptism,* two views, especially, have asserted themselves, views so common that we must take them up for discussion at this point before we proceed.

The one emphasizes quite correctly that Baptism is the means whereby the little one is regenerated. From the moment of Baptism the child has life in God. And now comes the Word as the means whereby the baptismal life which the little one possesses is, through the nurturing and guiding work of the Word, to unfold its indwelling vitality.

And wherever the Word is permitted to do its work through the Christian home, the Christian school, and the Christian church, there the baptismal life will grow quietly. Yet it is different with different people. In some it grows vigorously and quickly; in others, on the contrary, slowly and wretchedly. It may grow very differently, also, at different times in the life of the individual. During certain periods, both in childhood and in adult age, he may be laid hold of strongly and live a rich life in God. At other times the influence of the world may be stronger, so that his religious interests are weakened, and he may even forget God.

This view, however, has no use for and does not allow for awakening and repentance. The life in God has not died out. The baptismal life-germ lies in the depths of the soul. It is merely overgrown with worldliness and needs only to be dug out again. The Word is to do that. And the Word can do this in the easiest and simplest way by speaking to these worldly Christians about their Baptism and telling them that they *are* the children of God from the moment of Baptism. In this way these thoughtless people will most quickly be brought to see how they have neglected their God-life, and then they will begin to tend and care for it again.

This view cannot recognize awakening and repentance in the sense of *a decisive break* with the past life. Such a break or complete turning about would be fundamentally opposed to the view itself, namely, that the baptismal life in this worldly person never has died out. Here there can be no break, but only one line of life, which may indeed wind often in its course, but which never breaks.

The usual preaching of awakening and repentance is considered a foreign element which has gained entrance into the Lutheran Church, and is looked upon

as an incursion from the Reformed Church through
pietism.

On the basis of this fundamental principle it is
natural that the function of the Word with regard
to those who are baptized is conceived of as being
educational. Through the Christian influence of the
home, the school, and the church, the object is to
encourage, prompt, guide, admonish, discipline, and
chasten this child of God, according to its behavior
at all times, whether child or adult, either as a good
and obedient child, willing to learn, or as a recalci-
trant child of God.

And since the important point in all bringing up
is to appeal to the best in the child, it is essential that
the fact be understood as clearly as possible, that this
baptized person *is* the child of God. In this way he
himself will most easily come to realize how unreasonable it is to act toward God and man as he does.

For that reason the opinion is held that the preaching which speaks of these people as dead and as back-
sliders from God is both *unpedagogical* and *unpsychological*. It will only discourage these disobedient children of God, bewilder them, and in that way perhaps
even prevent them from rising from their disobedience and obstinacy.

As in all other bringing up, the quiet influence of
the home, school, and Church through good, inspir-
ing examples and wholesome habits of living is also

here the most effective. The child is to be led into the common religious life of the Christian home through family devotions, family singing, and a sound Christian home life. In like manner, it is to be accustomed early to take part in the children's services. And in due time it is to enter into the Christian work of the Church in which it comes natural for it to participate at all times.

And too great demands should not be placed upon the religious life of these people. Even though they are as yet pretty worldly, we should accept their assistance in Christian work with joy and gratitude because it is just this work which will bind them to Church and Christianity, and give them more strength to oppose the temptations of worldliness. The confidence which is thus placed in them will be a mighty moral lever in this as well as in all bringing up.

*

The other view of the relation between Baptism and the Word has not been analyzed so well nor made plain to the intellect. It is, therefore, more difficult to present. But, at all events, the gist of it is, that it places such a strong emphasis upon awakening and repentance that it cannot allow of a real regeneration in Infant Baptism. It does not aim to deny this article of our faith; nay, it is not even conscious of being in disagreement with the Confessions.

But it emphasizes so strongly that the real life in
God is attained primarily through the awakening and
converting effect of the Word that the regenerative
effect of Baptism is pushed aside in consciousness.
Baptism is never mentioned except every time it is
desired to admonish the hearers against the dead faith
which goes to sleep on Baptism.

What conception of the gracious effect of Baptism
is thus held, it is, as has already been mentioned,
not easy to say. But, consistently carried out, such
preaching will lead to this, that Baptism is not considered regenerative, but only a part of God's preparatory grace, which, like the preparatory effect of the
Word, aims at the awakening and conversion of the
one who is baptized.

According to this view, the relation between Baptism and the Word is, then, that the Word supple-
ments and completes the gracious work begun by
Baptism. Regeneration is therefore logically relegated
to the time of conversion.

*

In trying to decide with respect to these two views,
we shall begin by taking sides with the first-mentioned
in this, that it emphasizes so strongly the regenerative effect of Baptism in the child. This established
truth must not be altered, either because of difficulty
in *understanding* the regeneration of the child or be-

cause of difficulty in reconciling it with the preaching of awakening and repentance.

The child is born anew in Baptism. And this birth is, like every birth, an occurrence which cannot be supplemented afterwards. In Baptism the child becomes a true child of God.

But in regard to the relation between Baptism and awakening and repentance, we must dissent from the first-mentioned view.

We must, in the first place take exception to the idea that a baptized person retains a living germ of the baptismal life within itself also when he is living in sin without acknowledging it and without honestly confessing it. This idea is nothing but the human intellect's attempt to speculate about these inner psychological conditions without keeping to the safe ground of Scripture.

If we will let Scripture guide us also in this, we shall get the definite information that only they who have the Son have the life. "He that hath not the Son of God *hath not the life*" (1 John 5:12). "If any man love the world, the love of the Father is *not in him*" (1 John 2:12). "Whosoever therefore would be a friend of the world *maketh himself an enemy of God*" (James 4:4). "Every branch in me that beareth not fruit, *he taketh it away*" (John 15:2). "This my son was *dead,* and is *alive again*" (Luke 15:24).

The Word is to accomplish awakening and repentance in these baptized people who through conscious, unacknowledged, and unopposed sin have put to death the life with God which they received in Baptism. And that is the true meaning of these words: they must as dead be awakened from the dead. And they must *break* with their worldly life and *turn completely about,* leave the broad way, and enter upon the narrow one.

We shall touch upon the more intimate relation between this effect of the Word and baptismal grace more in detail in the selection dealing with the conversion of the backslider.

We must, in the second place, take exception to the first-mentioned view also as regards the work of the Word in those baptized persons who remain in their baptismal grace. The life which the child received in Baptism needs not only the nurture and guidance of the Word. It needs also the awakening and converting work of the Word. I shall now try to show how the baptismal life of the child is unable to lay aside its childishness and pass over into adult life with God unless the Word leads it through *awakening* and *repentance.*

In the child as well as in the adult, the Word is to clear away the hindrances which prevent the powers of grace received in Baptism from developing their indwelling life and doing their work of creating anew the one who is baptized.

These hindrances lie in the child as well as in the adult principally in the conscious life.* For that reason the gracious work of the Word is necessary as soon as the conscious life begins to awaken, because these hindrances assert themselves immediately. By way of a beginning, let us sum up briefly the awakening and converting work of the Word thus:

The work of the Word in the child as well as in the adult is to assist it

(1) to *see* these hindrances,

(2) to *will* to overcome them,

(3) to *be able* to overcome them.

In the first place, then, the Word is to awaken the child to see how it itself prevents the regenerating powers of Baptism from unfolding themselves. And since the hindrances lie in the inborn evil nature, which the child received at birth, therefore the Word must convince the child with respect to this inborn evil vitality.

This work of the Word in convincing the child of this must, of course, proceed slowly and gradually. But from the very beginning we must keep our goal in view. And the goal in the acknowledgment of sin is:

---

*In a previous section I have shown some of the hindrances which lie in the child's *unconscious* life, and have pointed out the most important ways by means of which we can help the child to get these hindrances cleared away even before the conscious life awakens.

(1) The definite break in the heart with all *conscious* sin,

(2) The humble acknowledgment of the wickedness of the indwelling nature, with its love of sin and its enmity toward God, and, thereby, the acknowledgment of total helplessness, so that the soul will trust alone in the forgiving and regenerating grace of God.

Now this acknowledgment occurs in the child only in an incomplete form, a fact which many parents do not recognize. They seek, therefore, in their well-meant zeal for the child to force an acknowledgment of sin for which the child as yet is not spiritually mature.

Throughout its whole childhood the child is unable to reach farther than to what is mentioned above in the first paragraph: to acknowledge and break with all *conscious sin*. And neither do the conscious sins include very much in the case of the child, at least to begin with. As yet it is able to acknowledge as sin just a few things: especially disobedience to parents, naughtiness toward brothers and sisters, telling lies, and saying bad words.

With regard to the last two of these, it is necessary to be very careful with the child in the beginning. It is not so easy for the child, to begin with, to distinguish between what it has seen and heard and what it has been imagining. For that reason we can often catch it telling falsehoods, and we are easily inclined to punish it for telling a lie. We must be careful about this in early years and not undertake to punish before we have assured ourselves that the child has spoken contrary to what it knows to be right.

In regard to bad words, too, the child may, to begin with, be entirely innocent. It has heard these bad words out among older children or adults, and they are repeated in all innocence. In that case it is essential for us not to punish the child, but to instruct it, and at the same time turn its attention away from these words.

Now the problem for us is to help the child to see *more* and *more* of such sins as a child is able to recognize as sin. But here, too, it is necessary to proceed according to the laws of pedagogy, and not burden the child with moral precepts which it is as yet not mature enough to grasp.

We should, meanwhile, not only help the child to see and recognize more sins; we should above all help it to gain a *deeper* conception of *sin itself*. For that reason, we must try to direct its thoughts inwardly to the root of sin, the sinful mind. This is not easy. Nevertheless, there are certain sinful *thoughts* which the child can quickly recognize as sin, namely its thoughts when angry, bitter and hateful thoughts; likewise envious thoughts; later also vain and am-

bitious thoughts; and, finally, toward the end of childhood, unchaste thoughts, when the sexual desires are
aroused and the child begins to indulge in these desires
in an impure thought-life.

Most important for us all in acknowledging sin is
unfeigned sorrow because of *sin itself* and not merely
on account of its *consequences*. We should therefore,
seek to develop in the child deep and sincere regret
because it has grieved Jesus by its sins. This is un-
doubtedly the most difficult problem in pedagogy. And
in solving it we must make use of all the means at
our disposal.

When the child has done something wrong, and
you discipline it, you must above all have the child
understand how grieved you are because of its sin.
For that reason you must never discipline the child
when you are wrought up with anger. In that case
you will create *fear* in the child, but not *regret*. On
the contrary, when you discipline the child, you must
show it that it grieves you to punish it, and above
all that you are sorry that it has sinned. If it is natural
for you to cry, let the child see your tears. They will
burn themselves into the soul of the child, and be
effective as long as it lives.

When you have disciplined the child, at least when
you have disciplined it more seriously than usual, you
should always bring the discipline to a close by kneel-
ing, helping the child to pray to Jesus for forgiveness.

You pray first. Then let the child pray afterwards. And when that has been done, you are to *declare* to the child the forgiveness of sins. Then you should draw the little one to yourself, and tell it that it has now received forgiveness from you; and Jesus, too, has forgiven it, so that everything is forgotten and all is well again. And Jesus will help the little one to be good and not do this again.

If this procedure is followed, the child's conscience will little by little be bound to Jesus, and thus its relationship to God will become something more than pious feelings during the moments of prayer. The little one should learn to know that it is bound in its conscience to Jesus *before* sinning, and *after* sinning to feel deep regret at having grieved Jesus.

If we succeed in this respect in bringing up the child, it will little by little become inwardly mature for the more independent life with God which in a natural way grows out of the child's dependency upon father and mother. In *early* childhood the child should cling to its parents both religiously and morally. But in *later* childhood it should little by little be inwardly released from this dependency and begin to associate in private with God and not only together with others at family devotions and evening prayers.

This can be accomplished in the simplest and most natural way by developing the conscience in the way I have just sketched. The result will be that the child

itself will feel a desire to speak alone with Jesus about
these things in which it has grieved him. And it is,
indeed, one of our happiest experiences with our children when we for the first time receive assurance
that the little one *alone* has sought Jesus to make up
with him and receive forgiveness.

In this way the child is also naturally led to use the
Word of God without help from others. And we should
provide our children with New Testaments as soon
as they have learned to read. To begin with we should
assign them how much they should read each day.
For it is essential that little children be given *definite*
assignments; otherwise it will all appear insurmount-
able to them, and they will quickly grow tired.

Along this way the child will also finally be led
to seek help through conversation about its little life
in God. We must ask God for this intimate confidence. And if we have received it, we must on our
knees pray to God every day that we may retain it.
For in the first place, it is most blessed both for the
parents and for the child. And, in the second place,
it is of inestimable value for the child during the difficult transition years.

Even as the child's knowledge of sin is both incomplete and immature throughout all of childhood, so,
too, is its knowledge of grace. The child does not
have the prerequisites necessary in order to apprehend
the innermost and the deepest things in the grace of

God, just because it does not as yet know the deep
root of its sin, namely, the heart's love of sin and
enmity toward God.

The element of grace which the child can grasp
is God's willingness to forgive sin, that he helps the
child to resist temptations, and helps it also in other
things, both great and small. There are parents who
have not understood this, and who have wanted to
compel their children to see their inner depravity and
know the grace of God like adults. And they have,
thereby, against their own will and without realizing
it, injured the religious development of their children, and in many instances driven their children
away from God.

*

Before we leave the age of childhood and pass on
to the transition years, we must first take up the question of *children* who have fallen away from their baptismal covenant.

First a few words concerning the falling away of
children in general. As mentioned above, there is a
camp which denies that a baptized child can fall away
from God. They maintain that the life which the little one received in Baptism does not die out even
though the child does not seek God in prayer and in
the reading of his Word, and does not honestly acknowledge and struggle against its sin. This view,

however, is contrary to Scripture, as shown above.
And we must hold fast that the passages of Scripture cited above apply to both children and adults.

Concerning the falling away of children, let us first
remind ourselves by way of consolation that a baptized child *cannot* fall away from God as long as it
lives only in the unconscious life. Secondly, in the
early part of the child's conscious age it cannot *of
itself* break with God. If the baptismal life of the
child dies during these years, it is the fault of the
parents. In that case they have neglected to give the
child's God-life the nature and guidance which it
needed as soon as the conscious life began to awaken.

In the third place, about midway between the age
of two and the transition from child to adult, the
child reaches a conscious, volitional life developed to
such a degree that it has the necessary psychological
qualifications for determining its own childlike relation to God. At that age the child itself *can* break
with God.

Concerning the marks which indicate a falling away
in children, we must, on the one hand, observe that
both in the case of the child and of the adult it is a
question of the inner life, and not merely of outward
religious forms, such as prayer, reading, and attend-
ance upon services. It depends upon the attitude in
which the child performs these religious exercises. Of
course, we cannot expect the same mature mind as in

grown persons. Everything is done in a childish way. Proof that there is life in the religious exercises of the child is this, that the child sincerely confesses to God the sins of which it is conscious in its childhood stage of development. The child that lives in conscious sins, without acknowledging and struggling against them, has fallen away from God even though it prays and reads the Bible.

Meanwhile, it is necessary to be aware of the child's dependency upon the Christian guidance of its parents. As mentioned above, the parents should take the child with them to the Lord and help the child to ask him forgiveness for its sin. I would, therefore, express the relationship thus: that child has fallen away from God which *will not* from the heart ask God's forgiveness for the sins of which it is conscious when the parents seek to have the child kneel and make up with God.

If a child has thus fallen away from God, we should speak the Word of God to it for the purpose of leading it to *awakening* and *repentance*. True, there are some who think that this is unnecessary. They think that we should rather try to speak to the child about Jesus so that it will again be induced to love him, and be good at home as well as away from home. But this line of thought is both unbiblical and unpsychological both as concerns children and grown persons.

Faith is always psychologically conditioned by *re-*

gret and *reconciliation.* Thus it is in life even between people. If I have offended a person, a *confidential* relationship between us cannot be restored before I am willing to confess my offense against him, even though he is willing to forgive me.

For that reason we must speak to the fallen child for the purpose of leading it to awakening and repentance. It is a distortion of the Gospel to tell these children that Jesus is just as pleased with them. On the contrary, we should tell them that Jesus grieves over them. And we should tell them of their sin, namely, that they do not care to have Jesus watch over their daily life and that they will not heed the reproach of their conscience. But at the same time we must tell them how Jesus desires to save them from this wicked and untruthful life. We should tell them about the suffering and death of Jesus for them. Nothing else is so certain to melt the defiance and obstinacy of the little heart. And we are to tell them that Jesus is just waiting for them to come and tell him things as they are: for then he is willing to forgive all.

But this must be made known to the child *in a childlike way,* a condition which many overlook in the home and in the Sunday school.

C. In the Transition Period

I now desire to speak of the *God-fearing* child's religious transition from child to adult.

It became a child of God in Baptism. And it has lived as a child of God ever since, in childish acknowledgment of and opposition to all conscious sin. Jesus says about the little child that in its relationship to God it is a model for us grown people. Some might, therefore, ask if this child needs to experience a special awakening and repentance during the transition from child to adult.

To this may be replied that the God-life of the child is indeed a model for us adults when viewed *from one side*. But at the same time, viewed *from another side,* there is something *incomplete* and *imperfect* about the God-life of a child. Paul expresses it thus: "When I was a child, I spake as a child, I felt as a child, I thought as a child: now that I am become a man, I have put away childish things" (1 Cor. 13:11). And we shall now try to show what takes place when the God-fearing child puts away the childish things in its life with God.

＊

We have noted that the God-fearing child gradually gains a *deeper* conception of its sin. How rapidly this development may progress is dependent mainly upon two factors, a subjective and an objective. The *first* is that the child receive the necessary guidance from parents or others concerning the will of God. We should note, however, that this guidance is not to be given

in words only, but also in a holy life which the child
can see every day. *Secondly,* that the child is scrupu-
lously honest and that it conscientiously follows the
little light which it has at all times been able to see.
In that case it will go from light to greater light wonderfully fast.

Its knowledge will, in that case, very early progress
inwardly from wicked deeds and bad words to the
attitude of mind. There is nothing to prevent a ten-
year-old child from beginning to see and to struggle
against the sins of the mind.

The child's battle against sin is thereby transferred
to a different plane. To struggle against sin in word
and deed may be hard enough for the child. But to
combat sinful thoughts, the sins of the mind, is
many times as hard. And what makes the battle especially hard is this, that the child now begins to notice the sins of *omission,* not only the sins of *commission.*

It sees now that God looks at the attitude of mind
back of the deeds. And the question soon arises which
is destined to destroy the God-fearing child's childish
peace: *"Do you love God?"* You pray; you read the
Bible; you go to church. That is true. But do you do
it because you love God? Do you hate sin? You struggle against sin, to be sure; but do you do it because
you hate sin?

To begin with, these questions will only bewilder the child. These thoughts are entirely new. The child knows neither what to think nor what to do. This, too, is a step in God's gracious leading of the God-fearing child. It will serve to remove the superficiality and cocksureness with which as a child it decided everything, also things religious. At the same time it serves to give the child an unconscious or semiconscious feeling of total helplessness.

As the child continues working candidly with these questions, it will be compelled to say to itself: "I do not hate sin. At heart I love it, but I dare not commit it because I am afraid of the temporal and eternal consequences. Of course, I can walk around envying my playmates who have the courage to indulge in their sinful desires. And since my attitude toward sin has become such, it is not at all strange that my relationship to God has gone to pieces. I pray, of course, and read the Bible also; but I do not do it because I love God. I do it because I know that those who desire to be Christians are supposed to do it. Possibly I do it most because I do not want Father and Mother to suffer the pain of seeing me quit. You know they have rejoiced so much because of my life with God."

When the child first begins to struggle with these questions, it suffers very severely under it and grieves bitterly because it has gone wrong inwardly. But after

some time it does not even feel this grief. It sees its
condition, but is no longer moved by it. The heart
has become cold and hard.

The baptized and God-fearing child's *awakening is
complete*.

What the child has now seen compels it to consider
itself a *fallen child:* only the outward *forms* of its
previous life in God remain. And these forms are
nothing but an abomination to God. The child knows
that it is baptized, and that it became a child of God
in Baptism. It knows, too, that it lived a happy life
with God during its childhood. But what good does
all this do now when it has lost its life in God, and
has only the form of godliness left?

*

Why does the God-fearing child have to go through
this experience? For the simple reason that it cannot
put away childish things and become a grown person in its relation to God in any other way. As I
pointed out above, it is the work of the Word to
show the baptized child the hindrances to its baptismal life which the child has within itself, namely
the evil nature which it received through its natural
birth.

This awakening work of the Word has been in
progress ever since the Word could begin to influence the child. But now for the first time the child

has reached that stage in its psychological development when the Word can complete the awakening,
that is, convince the child fully of the evil nature
with which it is endowed.

And let us also note that the child simply cannot
experience this awakening enlightenment of the Word
without being affected in the way I have shown. It
comes to see something which deprives it of every
hope of being in the right relation to God.

This experience is also necessary for the child, and
that not only because it needs to experience and acknowledge its indwelling *sin;* it is precisely to the
same degree necessary for the child's experience of
salvation. As pointed out above, the experience of the
child is just as incomplete and immature with regard
to sin as it is with regard to grace. Throughout its
whole childhood the child has never apprehended that
the grace of God is unmerited, because it has never
felt the root of sin in its mind, which does not love
God but loves sin.

On the other hand, the child has now gained such
a knowledge of its sin that it cannot get along with
its childish experience of grace. It must now also pass
over to a new plane in its experience of salvation and
the assurance of salvation. If grace is to do its work
in the child, then the child must experience it as unmerited grace, which it indeed is.

In Baptism the child becomes a partaker in the fullness of God's grace. But because of the child's psychological condition, grace has not as yet been able to do its complete work. The child has not been able to make use of more than a small portion of the grace it has received. But now, because of this experience of sin, it is able to experience the innermost essence of baptismal grace: its being unmerited.

It has now become clear to us that the awakening affects the God-fearing child in exactly the same way as it affects the grown person who has fallen away from God. It works in both a knowledge of sin that reaches into the heart's world, until both feel themselves perfectly helpless in the grip of sin, because they love sin and are unable to change this love.

The difference between awakening in the adult and awakening in the child is only a difference in length of time. In the child it takes at least from twelve to fifteen years, from the age of two, when the conscious life awakens, to the age from fifteen to twenty when the child passes over from childishness to maturity in its religious life. In grown persons it *is possible* for the awakening to come about more quickly because there is nothing in their psychological development which acts as a hindrance. But usually it takes several years, also in adults, even though they themselves are not conscious of it. See above in the section about the unconscious life.

When the awakening of the God-fearing child is complete, it necessitates a *choice*. This choice is unavoidable. But *what* it will choose is left to the child to determine.

If the child submits to the conviction it has gained through its awakening, it will experience *repentance*.

There are, to be sure, many who would not use the term "repentance" in mentioning this experience of the God-fearing child. But as far as I am able to understand, it is only a peculiarly stiff-necked dogmatism which prevents them from doing so. At least, their reasons cannot be logical or terminological ones. For what the God-fearing child now experiences is so precisely the same as the backslider experiences during his conversion that it is both natural and proper on logical as well as on terminological grounds to use the same term.

Of course, there is a difference. But it is of a *theoretic nature*. For the God-fearing child has not been off into the far country, as the backslider has. On that account it does not have such an outwardly sinful life to turn from. Let us, however, observe that the child certainly *feels* like a backslider. For that reason it experiences in its consciousness a choice between the two kinds of life, exactly like the backslider. Furthermore, the backslider's *real* battle during conversion is not against the outwardly coarse sins, but against what the Epistle to the Hebrews calls "repentance from dead works" (Heb. 6:1). Thus the struggle toward repentance becomes the same also theoretically for the God-fearing child as for the backslider.

There is indeed, a difference here both of an objective and of a subjective nature; but it is so immaterial for the choice in repentance that it really does not enter into consideration. I shall, nevertheless, mention it.

The God-fearing child is better situated than the backslider when it comes to *outward* sin. The God-fearing child has, of course, never been subject to this. It may have *fallen* into such sins. But it has never *lived* in them. It has had to confess them immediately and struggle against them. For that reason, these sinful habits have not had a hold on this child. The backslider, on the other hand, may often have had hard battles on this score. Many have abandoned themselves to a sinful life in drink and unchastity, falsehood and dishonesty. And as a result of habits extending over many years, sin secures such a grip on both body and soul that it means a life and death struggle for the slave of vice in order to be delivered from these sinful habits.

On the other hand, the backslider is more fortunately situated with regard to *inner sins*. Because of his outward sins he is so inwardly crushed that it is not so difficult for him to admit his total helplessness before God. He looks upon himself as a wreck, and to him it is nothing less than a miracle that God can receive him.

The God-fearing child, however, meets its greatest difficulty right here. Because of its pious life throughout all of childhood—and now, too, its outward life is pious and good—it is difficult for it to acquiesce in the judgment which the Spirit of God through the Word has passed upon its inner life. It is more easily tempted to evade the truth and rest satisfied with its Baptism and its pious life.

Indeed, this is the great *danger* for the God-fearing child during its struggle toward repentance.

In the first place, the whole thing is quite unintelligible to the child. The indolent flesh makes use of this inability to understand in order to tempt the child to let the whole thing go—it will all straighten itself out again. Or it will tempt the child to throw it all aside as a sickly notion: "Did you not become a child of God in Baptism? You have also lived as a child of God ever since. You have never desired to depart from God. Everybody considers you a child of God, too."

In this spiritual condition the child has but little strength with which to oppose sin. It no longer has peace with God in its soul and joy in the Lord as it had before. It is, therefore, powerless, and subject to all sorts of temptations. And if exceptionally strong

and enticing temptations come from without at this
time, this child may yield and openly fall from God.

This, however, occurs comparatively seldom. Most
God-fearing children who are unable to choose unto
repentance permit themselves to be led in another di-
rection. They compromise with their convictions. They
try to accommodate themselves to this new spiritual
condition. They admit that they are not *right* with
God as before. But they console themselves with the
idea that what they are now experiencing is the same
as grown people often speak of in connection with
their Christian life, namely, *attacks of spiritual doubt.*
Furthermore, the Scriptures say something about working out your own salvation with fear and trembling.
This fear and unrest which they have felt recently
are presumably a part of being a true Christian. And
thus they calm themselves.

This is so much easier because of the pernicious
pastoral care that is often exercised in such instances.
These young people who because of their piety have
been the pride of the home, the light of the school,
and the pastor's joy, go in their spiritual distress either
to their dear teacher or pastor and pour out their
hearts. Often, even before the anxious souls have had
time to tell all that pains them, the poor pastor begins
to offer consolation. As soon as he is certain that the
dear young child has not fallen openly, he pats him
on the shoulder and says: "My dear child, what are

you worrying about now? You have certainly always
been so good and honest both toward God and man
that you must realize that this is Satan's attempt to
embitter your life. Now do not worry any more over
this, but go home and thank God, who gave you the
good fortune to remain in the grace of your Baptism
and thus please both God and man by your upright
life."

*

Why cannot the God-fearing child keep its spiritual life by retaining its *former* piety? What is it that
causes its life with God to die now?

The answer is exceedingly simple: the God-fearing
child has now received *new* light. But it will not follow this light. And since this opposition to the Spirit
of God is not merely a fall which is regretted and re-
sisted, but develops into persistent obstinacy, the child
thereby puts to death the life in God which it has
had and in which it has lived from the moment of
Baptism.

Now it continues to live a life which it itself and
many *others* believe is a Christian life. It is of course,
almost as religiously disposed as it is possible to be,
by inheritance, by training, and by the religious life
which it has lived since Baptism. But the religious
life which it now lives after this crisis which we have
just described, is nothing but *the natural man's* reli-

gious life in all the Christian forms with which such
a God-fearing child is very familiar.

There are not a few of these religious people in
the congregations. And none cause the true believers greater difficulty than these. The ungodly and
secular world is much more kindly disposed toward
the believers. Inwardly the world has a holy respect
for people who take Christianity seriously. But these
self-righteous religious people are the worst and most
persistent enemies of the believers.

This is easily understood. There is something within them which becomes restless whenever they come
in touch with living Christianity. Then they are re-
minded that they swerved at the decisive moment.
Their persistent opposition to the true Christians finally becomes a war of defense, prosecuted on their own
behalf in order to make themselves and others believe
that the life they are living is real Christianity, while
the life of the believers is fanaticism and pietism,
a self-sufficient and arrogant, sectarian and factional
element within the church, which it is necessary to
keep in check.

When these people reach the point where they are
to choose their calling in life, and they really have
the opportunity to choose for themselves, they most
naturally decide upon a vocation which has something to do with religion. If they can become pastors,
they take that course. If they are unable to provide

themselves with the long and expensive education
which is necessary for this, they go to normal schools
and become teachers. In both these professions we
have had and still have many of these people who
will not tolerate living Christianity.

*

We have now followed the development of the God-
fearing child which will not submit to the humiliat-
ing conviction of truth brought on by the awakening. We shall now follow the development of the
child which submits.

It believes as mentioned above, that it has fallen
out of living fellowship with God and has only the
empty forms of life left. It sees its sinful heart which
loves sin and not God. It feels the hardness and in-
difference of its heart, and recognizes, therefore, that
it is totally lost. It also believes oftentimes, if not
always, that it has sinned against the Spirit. Has it
not "tasted the good Word of God and the power
of the world to come," and then failed God? It says,
too, that God will spew the lukewarm out of his
mouth. And when they are so cold and indifferent
now, it must be because the Spirit of God has for-
saken them.

But in this torture, too, they are honest. They cannot abandon themselves to sin. Neither can they begin to be dishonest with themselves. They confess hon-

estly to themselves and to God their true condition
and how they have deported themselves. And now
their little hard and obstinate heart is broken. They
have now lost all confidence in themselves, and therefore do not resist the unmerited grace of God any
longer. For that reason the unmerited grace of God
itself can now reach that heart. A short passage of
Scripture, explained by the Spirit of God, is sufficient
to cause the light to shine. The child now sees that
in order to be saved nothing more is necessary than
to be a sinner who will not conceal or spare any of
his sin. but surrender himself to him who justifies
the ungodly.

*

We have now followed the baptized, God-fearing
child up to the moment when, through awakening
and repentance, it has experienced grace unmerited
and received the full assurance of salvation through
faith in the righteousness of Christ.

But now our question recurs again: What is the
relation between Baptism and the Word? Of what
significance is it, in other words, to this child that it
is baptized?

This question gives rise to serious difficulties, and
that not only for the child who experiences what we
have just described. As a rule it is unable to get the
relationship clear in its mind. Perhaps during this

time its desire for a theoretical explanation is not so very pronounced either. That usually develops later.

The one who is to exercise spiritual care of a God-fearing child in the transition age will also feel the difficulty. How shall we orientate the child, so both Baptism and the Word will be rightly evaluated in its consciousness, and thus give the child all the help it so sorely needs during this critical period?

However, it is true here as in life generally: *life* solves the problems before the *mind does*. With instinctive certainty the child has taken the right position in this difficult situation, although it is by no means able to give the theoretical reasons for its position.

The child takes a very correct position, in the first place, to its Baptism, and that in spite of the wretched pastoral care it has received. It does not deny the gift of Baptism, that it really became a child of God in Baptism. But it does deny that its Baptism is proof that it is a child of God *today*.

In this respect the child's view is entirely correct and wonderfully clear. If the child should make use of its Baptism as a guaranty of its life in God, it would be exactly as absurd as if a believer should make use of his conversion as proof that he now has life in God. On the contrary, the child's view is right when it maintains the *previous* experiences of God's grace are not sufficient proof that it lives with God *now.* For it may have lost the gracious life which it once possessed. And that is exactly what the child thinks about itself.

The child also takes the same correct and clear position with regard to its God-fearing childlife. It does not deny that it has lived a happy life with God through all the years of childhood. But it denies that this is any guaranty that it now possesses this life in its heart. In this respect the child's view is marvelously clear, although it certainly is unable to substantiate its view theoretically. It is disengaging itself from the imperfection and incompleteness of its childish relationship to God. The basis of its childish *assurance* of the grace of God was the work of Christ *in its heart,* and it could not be anything else in that stage of its development. But now the time has come when its assurance no longer *can* rest upon this foundation.

This is the inner reason why the child must now look upon both Baptism and its God-fearing life in a new light. It begins now to see that Baptism does not save *ex opere operato,* that is, simply because of the administration of the act of Baptism. In this respect the child sees more clearly than the pastors and teachers mentioned above, who refer the child so anxiously to the fact that it is baptized. These people certainly are not conscious of how Catholic their whole view of Baptism is. They present it to the child as if the most important thing is that the act of Baptism has been performed upon them.

The child takes a much more biblical and Lutheran view of the matter. It sees that the administration of the act of Baptism is not what counts, but the attitude the child takes toward the salvation given in Baptism. The very moment it gives up building its assurance upon the fact that it is baptized and that it has lived a God-fearing life and surrenders its worldly, self-righteous and God-hating heart to him who justifies the ungodly, at that moment the child takes the right position with reference to its Baptism. Then, for the first time while fully conscious, the child receives the Baptismal gift as it really is, namely, as a gift of *grace*.

Now the child does not build upon the administration of the act of Baptism, nor on what Christ has done *in* the child; on the contrary, the child now clings to and builds its faith on what Christ has done *for* it. Thereby it has apprehended and appropriated to itself the true baptismal gift of salvation. For, as we saw above, the gift of Baptism is that it puts us in fellowship with the death and resurrection of Christ.

But even though the child thus in a practical way takes the right position with reference to Baptism, it may be, nevertheless, that it is unable to explain its relation to Baptism *theoretically*. And that is, of course,

a loss to the child in various ways, also in that it de-
lays the development from child to grown person
which we have just described. This process would
certainly take place more easily and quickly if the
child could receive this theoretical guidance concerning the relation between Baptism and the Word, between regeneration in Baptism and awakening and
repentance.

Then it would see that Baptism normally leads to
the awakening and repentance it now experiences. On
the other hand, it would see that the fellowship with
God, the assurance of salvation which it now experiences during its awakening and repentance, is neither
anything new nor anything else than the grace it received in Baptism; but that the grace of Baptism is
just what it has been put in condition to make use
of and *apply*. It can by no means receive *more* than
it *received* in Baptism; because at that time it received
fellowship with Christ and thereby a part in the full
propitiation which he made.

D. In Relation to the Conversion of the Backslider

Under the section above entitled *The Conscious Period of Childhood* I have given an account of two opposing views of the relation between Baptism and
the Word. The one holds that there is a hidden germ
of life from Baptism also in such as live in conscious
sins without confessing them and struggling against

them. I showed there that this view is contrary to
Scripture. I shall therefore not touch upon that here.
Let me simply postulate that the backslider must repent in order to be saved again (Eph. 5:14; 2 Tim.
2:25). And because he is *dead* he must be made *alive
again* (Luke 15:24).

The other view I presented gives no room for Baptism in its preaching, but relegates regeneration to
the moment of repentance in the case of both the
God-fearing child and the backslider. That the backslider was baptized as a child, this preaching mentions only when it desires to warn worldly people
against consoling themselves with their Baptism.

This preaching is, however, actuated by one right
motive which we must not overlook. It desires to get
away from the unbiblical thought that an abiding life-
germ from Baptism remains in the backslider. It desires to emphasize that the backslider is *dead* in his
trespasses and sins (Eph. 2:1-5). And, secondly, it
desires to emphasize that in repentance something
new is created in him, namely, the God-life which he
lost when he fell. It desires to emphasize that a *miracle
of salvation* takes place every time a backslider is converted.

But having hereby recognized what is justifiable
in this view, we must also point out its weakness. We
have here a misunderstanding of the dispensation of
salvation which the Lord ordained. And the misunder-

standing is quite extensive. It is a misunderstanding
of *Baptism,* of *regeneration,* of *repentance,* and of the
continuity in the work which God does unto salvation in the human soul. Let us now consider this
briefly.

*

The real gift of Baptism is, as we pointed out above,
to transfer to the individual the full salvation which
is in Christ. And God never takes back this transference of power. This side of Baptism has been expressed
thus by Gisle Johnson: "To be baptized means the
same as always to be in the washing of Baptism."

From the time of Baptism as much of this Christian life as the child is able to receive is transferred
to it every moment. And it becomes the Word's task
to clear away the hindrances to this transference of
power in the child, and thus provide more and more
room for these powers of salvation. Consequently, God
gives nothing more than he gave in Baptism. At that
time the child received Christ. And God has nothing
greater to give to sinners.

If a baptized person falls away from God, what happens then?

Then this person's living connection with Christ is
terminated. He is without life in God and therefore
dead and lost (Luke 15:24). But though this person

has turned away from the grace of Baptism, the grace of Baptism has not turned away from this person. God never takes back the baptismal transference of power from one who is baptized. But now after the fall the sinner shuts out God's saving power from his heart and his life. The sinner cannot, however, prevent grace from working upon him. It is shut out from his heart, but continues nevertheless to work upon his heart.

And this it does in various ways, both through consciousness and subconsciousness. The Word works upon the conscious life unto awakening and repentance. And down in the subconscious the psychological impressions which had accumulated before the fall away from God through the gracious effects of Baptism and the Word are at work all the time. Under the guidance of the Spirit, these subconscious psychological movements work toward a meeting with the conscious effects of the Word's message of awakening to the backslider.

Now when this fallen person repents, what takes place?

Nothing is changed from God's side. For he has never withdrawn the powers of salvation which he transferred to this sinner in the hour of Baptism. It was the sinner who through his fall refused to accept them. That was what occurred in the fall. And now through repentance a change occurs only on the side

of the sinner. He now chooses to allow these powers
of salvation to gain unhindered access to his soul and
body again.

What happens then?

Then these powers of salvation bring forth *the same
life* again as they brought forth in the hour of Baptism. At the moment of repentance the sinner's living
connection and living fellowship with Christ, which
had been terminated, are re-established. And Christ's
life pours again into him who during the whole period of estrangement was *dead*.

Then we usually say that he is *born anew*. The idea
in this expression is correct. We mean to say that a
miracle of salvation has taken place in the backslider.
Through the supernatural power of God he has been
translated from death to life. But the expression is an
unfortunate one. It is neither logically nor biblically
permissible. For we speak of a *birth* only the first
time a person receives life. If a person who is born
dies and receives life again, he is not *born* once more,
but is *raised from the dead* as, for instance, Lazarus
and the Widow of Nain's Son.

The same mode of expression will, therefore, be
natural in the realm of spiritual life. A person who
has been born anew once, that is, has received the life
in God, but who loses this life and recovers it, of him
it is not natural to say that he is born anew still an-

other time. We would rather say of him that he is
raised from the dead.

And this is exactly the expression used in Scripture.
As far as I know, Scripture never speaks of a fallen
Christian who again repents and receives the life in
God, as one who at that time is born anew once more.
On the contrary, Scripture says that he is raised from
the dead. "Awake, thou that sleepest, and *arise from
the dead,* and Christ shall shine upon thee" (Eph.
5:14). As is well known, these words are directed
to the believers who had fallen away from fellowship
with God. Of these it is written that in order to be
saved again they must arise or be awakened from
the dead. Jesus also says the same about the Prodigal
Son: "This my son was dead, and is alive" (Luke
15:24).

By means of this scriptural terminology we are
able to bring out more easily the right relation between Baptism and the word at *this* point. Here we
do not have only the misunderstanding that has been
mentioned, that the Word is the real means of regeneration and that Baptism is only a part of preparatory grace. Many, also of those who hold fast to Baptism as a means of regeneration, become confused with
regard to the relation between Baptism and the Word
when it concerns the salvation of the backslider. They
think that we have two means of regeneration, name-

ly, Baptism and the Word. And they determine the
relation between them thus: Baptism regenerates *all,*
whether they are baptized as infants or as adults. The
Word, on the other hand, regenerates only such as
have fallen away from the life which they received in
Baptism.

To substantiate this line of thought they cite a
number of passages from Scripture which say that regeneration is accomplished by means of the Word of
the Gospel. "Having been begotten again through the
Word of God" (1 Peter 1:23). "Of his own will he
brought us forth by the word of truth" (James 1:11).
"For in Christ Jesus I begat you through the Gospel"
(1 Cor. 4:15).

But to understand these words thus is impossible.
In the first place, we have already seen that Scripture
does not speak of regeneration but of the awakening
of the dead when a baptized person again comes to
life in God. Scripture speaks, then, of regeneration
only when a person for the first time comes to life
in God. And that takes place according to Scripture
through Baptism. (See what has been said above regarding Baptism as a means of regeneration in the
section dealing with *The Baptismal Gift of Salvation.*)

What, then, is meant when Scripture speaks of regeneration by means of the Word or the Gospel? Let
us first observe that no other regeneration is meant

than the one which takes place in the moment of Baptism; for Scripture does not know of more than this
one regeneration.

In the next place, let us observe how we *create* difficulties by our interpretation of Scripture, namely,
by a spiritless bondage to the letter of Scripture. When
James, Peter, or Paul says that the readers are regenerated by the Word, we read it as though there were
added: and not by Baptism. Then the difficulty begins. To the apostles, on the other hand, there was
no difficulty regarding the relation between Baptism
and the Word. We see that plainly from their writings. These deal with many difficult questions for the
benefit of their readers. But they never discuss this
question. From this we can conclude that the question never caused them any difficulty.

To be begotten again by the Word and to be regenerated through Baptism are to the apostles one and
the same thing, only viewed from different sides, expressed in different ways. We must accustom ourselves
to this, that the apostles speak of that side of the matter which interests them in a certain connection, without mentioning the other sides of the matter, which
they have spoken of in other places. To the apostles
it is self-evident that the Word and Baptism work
together. The Word brings forth faith (Rom. 10:7).
But faith is not built on air. Faith is faith in the Gospel (Mark 1:15). But the Gospel is not something dif-

ferent from Baptism. The Gospel also contains the
words of Jesus about Baptism. Therefore, no one can
believe the Gospel without seeking Baptism immediately (See Acts 2:41). To desire and to receive Baptism become, therefore, the first testimony that the
Gospel has brought forth faith.

As a result of this, Baptism and the Word are not
in the New Testament looked upon as being opposed
to each other, but as being intimately associated with
each other. Baptism is a part of the Gospel, a part of
the glad tidings. For that reason the apostles can say
that we are begotten again by the Word, especially
in places where they according to the context are not
interested in separating or speaking individually of
the parts employed by the Gospel of Christ. On the
other hand, wherever according to the context they
wish to give expression to the peculiar nature and
effect of Baptism, there they say that Christ has joined
the saving and regenerating work of the Spirit to the
washing of Baptism. (See the section above concerning *The Baptismal Gift of Salvation.*)

*

Before I leave this section, I shall try to illustrate
the relation between Baptism and the Word by means
of a figure from the realm of mechanics.

The wire is put into our house from the electric

power station. As soon as the wire is installed and the power is turned on, it is only a question as to whether the contacts are in order in the house; if so, the power quietly does all its work, gives light and heat, cooks, fries, and bakes, washes, dries, and irons.

If the contacts are destroyed in one way or another, the power ceases to work at once. It becomes cold and dark, and all machines stand still. But the wire leading into the house is exactly the same as before. And the power from the station is on. Now in order to make the repairs the station does not run a new wire into the house. The bad contact is simply repaired, and the power takes its usual course into the house and does exactly the same work as before: gives light and heat, cooks, etc.

The figure is commonplace, but let me apply it nevertheless.

In the hour of Baptism God laid the wire into the little child's soul. From that moment "the power is on." It accomplishes in the child all that the child has "contacts" enough to receive. The Word will see to it that there are more and more contacts in the child's soul to receive and to utilize all the power to which it has received access through Baptism.

Now when a baptized person falls away from God, nothing is changed in the "wiring." The power is on as before. It is only the contact in the soul which

has been destroyed. For that reason it has become
dark and cold in there, and all the activity of the
spiritual life has been stopped.

When a fallen person is awakened and brought to
repentance, no change takes place in the wiring or
in the amount of power. That is all exactly the same
as before. The change which occurs at repentance
takes place only within the person. The contact is
put in order again. The living connection with Christ
is re-established. There is light in the soul again immediately; heat likewise. And the activity of the new
life is again exactly the same as before the fall.

V

Importance for Preaching

AFTER this inquiry into the relation between the gracious effect in man of the Word and of Baptism, we shall now, lastly, note briefly how important it is for our preaching and our pastoral care to present these thoughts.

AS TO THE AWAKENING

Now it is not difficult to see that these thoughts will easily grip the soul and cause it to reflect. As long as the God-life appears to the unsaved person as something distant and strange and practically unattainable, he will continue the more easily to live his sinful life in peace, undisturbed. If, on the other hand, he begins to see that he did possess life in God during the first and happiest years of his life, life in

God will no longer appear as something distant and
strange. Memories of this childhood life with God
will be called forth, memories which have a peculiarly
attractive power because they stir the emotional life
in the same way as in the happy days of childhood,
and the sinner thereby receives the psychological prerequisites for feeling his worldly and God-distant life
as something strange.

Furthermore, if the sinner can only be brought to
see what he has once *possessed,* he will the more easily discover what he has *lost,* and feel how empty his
life is without God. Holy longings will be awakened.
The conscience will thereby gain a powerful ally deep
down in the sinner's soul.

But above all, never will the enmity of the sinner's
will toward God be more easily broken than when
he sees the mercy of God in the grace of Baptism,
namely, that the sinner can never change God's part
in the covenant of Baptism. With all his sin he cannot alter God's transference of power begun in Baptism. With all his recalcitrance he cannot change the
gracious will of God, by means of which he seeks
and influences the sinner every moment, whether the
sinner understands it or not and whether he desires
it or not.

God's tender care and patient perseverance with the
sinner in his frivolous and stubborn life will more
certainly than anything else overcome the sinner and

make his life so bitter and burdensome that he will
not be able to endure it any longer.

AS TO REPENTANCE

If the foregoing thoughts are of such importance
for a person's awakening, we can be more brief in regard to repentance. They will, in the first place, *spur
him on* to a choice, because they make his life in sin
burdensome to him and call forth deep longings for
the peace with God which he possessed during his
childhood years.

In the second place, these thoughts will to a large
degree *simplify* the choice for the sinner. And this
is of tremendous importance at this time. Everything
seems so impossible to him. How can he receive power
to become a different man and break with his old
life in sin? Here he learns that God will give him
this power. But how can he secure it? In truth, the
power wires have been in order since the moment of
Baptism. He broke the contact by falling away from
God. And now in repenting there is nothing that
he can do but to give Jesus the chance to use his power
within his helpless soul.

AS TO FAITH

This view of Baptism is none the less important
for faith. The great difficulty for the honest, awakened
soul is to believe the promises of God. He does *not*

doubt that the promises of God are true, but thinks
that they can never apply to him. He always dis-
covers something about himself which makes the
promises inapplicable to him, even though they apply
to all others. It cannot be denied that there is something *general* about the promises. They speak to all,
and do not address themselves so clearly to the individual, at least so it seems to the troubled soul.

In this respect Baptism occupies a peculiar position.
Baptism is *individualized grace*. Baptism is the most
distinct expression of the love of God for the individual. The promises of God are never spoken to the
individual alone, but to all at one time. Baptism, on
the contrary is something that God does to the individual. When I was baptized, God performed the
act upon me and it concerned no one else but me.
In order to be of greater help to the sinner, God has
met him not only with *words* spoken to him as an
individual, but in an *act*. And this act is to stand at
the beginning of our life and tell us more forcefully
than any word that God has once for all granted us
his grace. And he never takes it back. For that reason we retain it as long as we ourselves do not deny
it access and shut ourselves out from it. If we have,
through backsliding, shut ourselves out from it, we
can receive it into our lives again the moment we
ourselves will it so. For it only waits for us to give
it access.

ABOUT THE AUTHOR

Until his death in 1961, Dr. Ole Hallesby was one of Norway's leading theologians and occupied a position of unique importance in the land of his birth.

A man of deep convictions and evangelical fervor, he threw himself into the battle between liberalism and conservatism which raged in Norway during the 1920's and 1930's. He was a professor at the Independent Theological Seminary, Oslo, for 40 years and thus influenced hundreds of men who became pastors of the Church of Norway. During the Occupation of World War II, he became a figure of national stature in the resistance movement, working closely with the late Bishop Berggrav and other leaders in church and state.

Dr. Hallesby's influence on American Lutheran church life was also unique. He visited the United States only once—in the early 1920's. Through his books, however, he exerted an influence of almost unbelievable proportions. Nine of his 40 some books have been translated into English and published by Augsburg Publishing House.